MRS
BEETON
CAKES
& BAKES

Mrs Beeton How to Cook

Mrs Beeton Soups & Sides

Mrs Beeton Fish & Seafood

Mrs Beeton Chicken, Other Birds & Game

Mrs Beeton Classic Meat Dishes

Mrs Beeton Cakes & Bakes

Mrs Beeton Puddings

MRS BEETON CAKES & BAKES

ISABELLA BEETON
& GERARD BAKER

FOREWORD BY CLAIRE PTAK

For my grandmothers Nora Baker and Elsie Hinch,
who spanned the gap between Isabella and me.

Gerard Baker

This edition published in Great Britain in 2012 by Weidenfeld & Nicolson
Originally published in 2011 by Weidenfeld & Nicolson as part of *Mrs Beeton How to Cook*

1 3 5 7 9 10 8 6 4 2

Text copyright © Weidenfeld & Nicolson 2012
Design and layout copyright © Weidenfeld & Nicolson 2012

Design & Art Direction by Julyan Bayes
Photography by Andrew Hayes-Watkins
Illustration by Bold & Noble. Additional illustration by Carol Kearns
Food Styling by Sammy-Jo Squire
Prop Styling by Giuliana Casarotti
Edited by Zelda Turner

A CIP catalogue record for this book is available from the British Library.
ISBN 978 0 297 86681 7

The Orion Publishing Group's policy is to use papers that are natural, renewable and recyclable products and made from wood grown in sustainable forests. The logging and manufacturing processes are expected to conform to the environmental regulations of the country of origin.

Printed and bound in Spain

Weidenfeld & Nicolson
The Orion Publishing Group Ltd
Orion House
5 Upper St Martin's Lane
London WC2H 9EA

An Hachette UK Company

www.orionbooks.co.uk

CONTENTS

FOREWORD

A very gifted food photographer, who I worked with when I first moved to London, introduced Mrs Beeton's great work to me over a suet pudding and some clotted cream. He dropped her name into our conversation, as one might with Shakespeare or Dickens. I nodded knowingly, 'Yes, Mrs Beeton. Exactly'. Having never heard of her, I went home and did my research as soon as the shoot was over. Elizabeth David and Patience Gray had made it to the West Coast of America, but I had yet to discover the magnificent Isabella Beeton.

In 1861, this 25-year-old newlywed was a modern woman. She extolled the virtues of good food and a tidy house to make one happy and fulfilled and to, well, keep a husband. These may not sound like modern endeavors to our ears today, but she was revolutionary in that she recognised a need for this type of publication, and she made it available.

Beeton's Book of Household Management was for young women setting up a household of their own, written by a young woman doing just that. She maintained that a properly written recipe, using accessible, economical, and seasonal ingredients made sense because cooking good food at home would make your children happy and your husband want to spend more time there. I snigger at this one a little, but I think we do all want to make our partners and families happy, and baking a good cake accomplishes this almost every time.

I run my own bakery, Violet, in east London. I am a businesswoman and entrepreneur, but I also wear an apron most days. I think it is incredibly important to keep an organised and efficient kitchen – something Mrs Beeton was adamant about. If your fridge is in order, you know what is in it and therefore have a sense of what to shop for when out at the market. You will buy what is fresh and in season to supplement the store cupboard essentials. There will be less waste, because you are not buying things you already have and things will not go off. I also think baking can be wonderfully satisfying for the cook and consumer alike.

Perhaps the fact that Mrs Beeton was so far ahead of her time was what really drew me to find out more about her. She wrote her book at such a young age, with such gravitas. I love the way she often gave notes to her reader: like '[this] is easily accomplished', or 'not to be used incautiously'. She speaks with authority, but she assumes intelligence and common sense. A writer who understands her material and knows how to communicate it well never goes out of style.

Claire Ptak

THE INIMITABLE MRS BEETON

When Isabella Beeton first published *Beeton's Book of Household Management* in 1861, Britain was changing from a rural society, in which large numbers of people were involved in farming and many grew their own fruit and vegetables at home, to an industrialised one, where the development of modern transport networks, refrigeration and kitchen appliances brought a world of food to our fingertips.

Today, most of us have an image of Mrs Beeton as a matronly figure – brisk, efficient and experienced in the kitchen. In fact, Isabella Beeton was young and recently married, juggling working outside the home with running her household and coping with the demands of a husband and young family. Having worked on it throughout her early twenties, she saw her book published at the age of 25 and died just three years later.

Although she wrote of housekeepers, butlers and valets, her semi-detached in Hatch End was a world away from the big country houses of the preceding century, and although it is likely that she had some help in the kitchen, she almost certainly managed her home and most of the cooking herself. Her book was inspired by an awareness of the challenges faced by women like herself – and with that in mind, she used her position as editor of *The Englishwoman's Domestic Magazine* to pull together the best recipes and advice from a wide range of sources.

She was among the first revolutionary food writers to style recipes in the format that we are familiar with today, setting out clear lists of ingredients and details of time taken, average cost and portions produced (this last being entirely her invention). She also offered notes on how to source the best food for her recipes – placing particular emphasis on such old-fashioned (or, in our eyes, surprisingly modern) ideas as the use of seasonal, local produce and the importance of animal welfare.

It is easy to see why Mrs Beeton's core themes – buy well, cook well and eat well – are as relevant today as they were 150 years ago. Her original book was written with an awareness of household economy that we can take lessons from too. Because we have access to so much so easily, we often forget to consider how to get the most out of each ingredient – yet maximising flavour and nutrient value and minimising waste is as relevant in the twenty-first century as it was in 1861.

The right ingredients

Mrs Beeton's original recipes have needed careful adaptation. In some cases, the modern recipes are amalgamations of more than one Beeton recipe or suggestion, which I hope give a more coherent whole. Many of the ingredients that may seem at first glance universal are so different today from those varieties Isabella would have been familiar with that using them in the original way can give

quite different results to those intended. For those reasons, quantities needed to be not only converted but checked and altered. And all those cases where Mrs Beeton advised adding salt or sugar or honey or spices 'to taste' have been pinned down in real quantities, always keeping in mind both flavour and authenticity.

Cooking methods, too, were in some cases not replicable and in others simply no longer the best way of achieving the desired results. A significant factor in this is that the domestic oven was in its infancy in 1861, and Mrs Beeton was not able to make full use of it in her book. Most kitchens would instead have been equipped with old-fashioned ranges, and there is much mention of setting things before the fire, turning and basting. Baking or roasting, which we now consider simple processes, required constant attention 150 years ago. Oven temperatures, therefore, have all had to be deduced from a mixture of reading between the lines, comparing modern recipes, and testing, testing, testing.

The end result, however, has been to produce dishes that Mrs Beeton would, hopefully, have been happy to call her own.

The legacy

After Isabella Beeton died early in 1865, her book took on a life of its own. It was endlessly enlarged, modern recipes were added and eventually, in the many, many editions of the book that have been published in the past 150 years, the spirit of the original was lost.

The picture of British food that Isabella painted in the first edition was about to change wholesale, and her book was destined to change with it. The aim of this collection is to reverse those changes: to return to real, wholesome, traditional British food, which Mrs Beeton might be proud to recognise as her own – and to put to rest the matronly image.

INTRODUCTION

There is no denying that, as a nation, we have a sweet tooth. Walk down any high street today and bakeries still display a range of treats designed to tempt us inside. With a keen eye, you will find some British classics such as the pound cake, bara brith and Sally Lunn holding out against competition from supermarkets churning out muffins and cupcakes in astonishing variety.

Mrs Beeton was not an expressive or indulgent baker, whatever her reputation might suggest. Her cakes contained rather more flour and less sugar and butter than ours today, but it isn't difficult to work out why. She was a young woman running a household on limited resources. Clearly, money was not in plentiful supply. Nonetheless, she was keen to name butter as her fat of choice for baking – expensive as it was – and this sets a good example for us today.

Whatever you bake, your results will only be as good as the cheapest ingredient you use, so always aim high and buy the best ingredients you can afford. If you only allow yourself one piece of cake a week, you will want to make absolutely sure it is a very good piece of cake. And the best way to ensure that it is the best piece of cake ever is to have made it yourself.

Techniques

Creaming

The butter in cakes, such as the Victoria sandwich cake, is creamed. Here, softened, room-temperature butter is beaten with a wooden spoon or large whisk to add air. This lightens the butter's texture and colour. Once the butter has been beaten, sugar is added and the mixture beaten again, further lightening the mixture. Finally, egg is gradually beaten in resulting in a mixture that is shiny and glossy.

The main aim in creaming a mixture is to add the egg gradually and to beat the mixture thoroughly between each addition. This allows the egg and butter to be emulsified together properly, resulting in a mixture that holds air. If this emulsified mixture is broken, or curdled, a portion of the air is lost and the mixture will be heavier.

Whisking

This is the action of adding air to a mixture to lighten it in colour and texture. A metal balloon whisk is the best tool – either hand held or machine driven. Ingredients that are commonly whisked include eggs and cream. Properly whisked egg whites go through a dramatic transformation, first becoming frothy, and then turning pure white with a light and fluffy texture rather like shaving foam. The mixture should be able to hold its shape rather than running back into the bowl.

In some recipes egg whites are whisked on their own before being folded into the other ingredients; in others (for example when making meringues), they are whisked with sugar, which gives them a glossier appearance and a firmer set. A meringue mixture is often said to be able to hold 'stiff peaks'. Egg yolks, when whisked, will pale significantly in colour and increase in volume, but they will never hold their shape as firmly as egg whites.

Folding

The aim when folding two or more ingredients together is to limit the loss of air from the mixture, and this is a method used commonly in baking and dessert cookery. The best tool to use is a large metal spoon or spatula, using a gentle motion of folding one ingredient into the other to blend them – as opposed to beating them – together.

Kneading

The technique of mixing and working dough, usually made of flour, yeast and water, in order to make it into a cohesive, supple mass, is known as kneading. This can be done either by hand or using a machine. However, once you have brought the ingredients together with your hands to make the dough, you should leave it to rest for 20 minutes before kneading.

Kneading plain, white bread-flour dough

Place the rested dough on a lightly floured work surface, and flour your hands. Using one hand to anchor the dough in front of you, push the heel of your other hand into the dough, stretching it as you push it away from you. Use your fingertips to pull the leading edge of the dough back over the middle portion, forming a ball, and repeat this action.

As you knead, occasionally take a piece of dough the size of a golf ball and stretch it between the first and second fingers of both hands. The aim is to make a thin window-like sheet of dough that stretches without tearing until it is thin enough to see light through. You will notice that as you knead this becomes increasingly possible, and this is a sign that the dough is developing. If the dough tears when stretched, keep kneading.

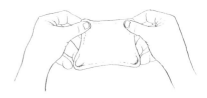

Kneading wholemeal bread-flour dough

Because wholemeal flour contains small pieces of wheat bran, it requires slightly different handling from white flour. It is even more important to leave the freshly mixed dough to rest before kneading for it to be able to develop properly. Knead the dough in stages, allowing it to rest for a couple of minutes occasionally before kneading it again. Do this over a period of 10–15 minutes.

When the dough (either plain white or wholemeal) is shiny and resistant but still very slightly sticky, it is fully developed. Now it can be left to rise in a large bowl in a warm place, covered with either a damp tea towel or oiled cling film.

Making yeast sponges for richer doughs

Bakers occasionally start a batch of yeasted dough using what is known as a 'sponge'. This is a loose batter made from a portion of the liquid, yeast and flour to be used in a recipe which will both give a deeper flavour and, especially when using spices, eggs or fat, a lighter texture because these ingredients tend to inhibit the action of the yeast.

Cooking Tips

Temperature and timing

The high sugar content of baked goods means that they are prone to overcooking if the heat is too fierce. Fan ovens (also called convection ovens) circulate hot air in the oven and so reduce cooking time. The timings in this section have been worked out using a fan oven. If yours is a conventional oven, raise the heat given in the recipes by 10°C, and expect the recipes to take slightly longer.

Where you place a tray of biscuits or a cake in the oven will affect how they bake, especially if you have a conventional oven. Place them too close to one side of the oven and they will cook unevenly. To prevent this, turn cakes and biscuits when they begin to brown so they colour and rise evenly.

Steam

Bread benefits from being baked in a humid, steamy environment. Steam slows down the formation of the crust, allowing the bread to rise more, producing a lighter loaf. You can introduce steam to the oven by placing a small roasting tin on the bottom of the oven when you first turn the oven on to preheat. Then add hot water to the tin just after you put the bread in. Be careful not to scald yourself with the steam, as it will rise violently when you pour the water in.

Lining cake tins

Cake or loaf tins are generally greased and lined before baking, even if they are non-stick. As well as making it easier to remove the finished cake or loaf from the tin, lining with baking paper makes tins easier to clean. Use melted butter, brushed into all the corners and edges of the tin, and then cut non-stick baking paper to fit. This paper is coated to prevent sticking – and is especially good when used with meringues, which tend to stick to aluminium foil or greaseproof paper.

Testing whether cakes and breads are cooked

To test whether a cake is cooked, insert a skewer into the centre and remove it. If it comes away clean, the cake is cooked. This method will not work for cakes that are intentionally left slightly undercooked for a fudgy effect, such as the dark chocolate cake on page 38.

To test whether a bread is cooked, slip it from its tin and tap the bottom gently with your knuckles. If the bread gives a hollow sound, it is cooked.

Alternatively, a temperature probe can be inserted into cakes and breads once they have reached the end of their cooking time. If a temperature of 95°C has been reached at the centre, the cake or bread is cooked.

Storing Baked Goods

Always store cakes and biscuits in airtight containers to stop them becoming stale. Butter-based cakes and biscuits keep very well, but they do eventually grow stale if not eaten. In the event that you end up with some stale cake, you can use it up in a queen's pudding (you can find a recipe for this in *Mrs Beeton Puddings*).

Bread goes stale quickly. Even the act of freezing bread seems to hurry it past its best. To extend its keeping time, wrap it well in a cloth bag and store it in a cool place.

PASTRY

Why Bother to Make Your Own Pastry?

It is almost impossible to buy good pastry, so if you want to eat the best, you must learn to make your own. Shop-bought pastry contains additives to make the pastry last longer on the shop floor. It also has any number of colour and flavour compounds to improve its appearance and taste, all of which would be unnecessary if the best ingredients were used in the first place.

Essentially, pastry is a mixture of flour, fat and water. The proportions of these ingredients can be altered to give different results, as can the type of fat and flour used (in addition, lemon juice is often added to pastry to make it crisper). You can, at a push, make pastry with almost any flour and fat, but all of your ingredients need to be looked after.

Flour

Freshness in flour is just as important as it is in fat. Flour that has been recently ground and well stored has a delicious fresh smell and runs easily through the fingers. It should feel dry and not cake in the hand when squeezed tightly. Old flour discolours and will smell rancid, like old fat. Avoid it.

Butter

Most of the butter we buy in the UK today is salted. Unsalted butter is easily available, but will not keep for as long. Pastry has a delicate flavour, so if you use salted butter in a recipe that calls for unsalted, remember to reduce the amount of salt added to the recipe to compensate.

Working and cooking temperatures

Because fat softens when warm, you must make pastry in cool conditions, using cool ingredients, unless a recipe says otherwise. Generally, if pastry becomes too warm when it is mixed (becoming sticky or oily), chill until dry again before adding any liquid, so that the balance can be maintained.

If the pastry is made with too little water (which is likely if it is too warm) it is said to be 'short' and will crumble. If too much water is added, the pastry will be sticky to handle and tough when baked.

Cooking temperature is also important. For perfect pastry, the oven temperature needs to be sufficiently high to cause the starch in the flour to expand and to set as the fat melts, so that the two can combine. If the temperature is too low when the pastry goes into the oven, the fat will melt and run from the pastry before the starch cooks, resulting in tough pastry.

When baking pastry blind, for example, for a tart case, the pastry must be allowed to dry once set, otherwise the bottom of the tart will be soft and flabby. To ensure that the pastry is properly cooked remove the baking beans and finish cooking the pastry at a lower temperature to ensure it cooks thoroughly and evenly before any filling is added.

SHORTCRUST PASTRY

✳ Makes enough for 1 x 22–25cm pie ✳ Preparation time 10 minutes plus 1 hour chilling time

Shortcrust pastry is used for all pies, tarts and small pastries, both sweet and savoury. It is the simplest pastry of all and can be made using butter, lard, dripping or suet, or any combination of these. Mrs Beeton gives several recipes for an everyday pastry, varying the proportion of fat to flour to suit the purpose. However, this simple half-fat-to-flour recipe is really all you need ever use. A little lemon juice added to the mix gives a crisper result.

250g plain flour

pinch salt

125g cold unsalted butter, cubed or grated

½ tsp lemon juice

100ml iced water

If you have a food processor, sift the flour and salt into the bowl and mix. Add the cubed butter and pulse until the mixture resembles fine breadcrumbs. Pour the mixture into a bowl.

If you are working by hand, sift the flour and salt into a bowl and add the cubed or grated butter. Rub the butter and flour between your fingertips until it resembles fine breadcrumbs, working quickly to keep the mixture as cool as possible. If it starts to feel sticky, chill the mixture for 30 minutes before moving on to the next step.

Add the lemon juice to the water and pour two-thirds of this into the flour mixture. Blend well with a fork, stirring quickly but gently. Using your fingertips, bring the dough together. Add more water as necessary (you may need to use all of it) until everything is evenly mixed and there are no dry lumps of flour. Bring the mixture together into a smooth, supple lump. Carefully form the pastry into a flattened ball, wrap in cling film and chill for at least 1 hour before using.

FLAKY SHORTCRUST PASTRY

✳ Makes enough for 1 x 22–25cm pie ✳ Preparation time 10 minutes plus 1 hour chilling time

Mrs Beeton gives a recipe for a 'medium puff paste' that is a halfway house between shortcrust and puff pastry, but made in the same way as puff pastry. The recipe here achieves the same result with far less fuss. A portion of the fat is blended with the flour mixture while the remainder is added in small lumps. These melt as it bakes, giving the resulting pastry a delicious, yielding flakiness. This pastry is excellent for using in fruit or other pies.

250g plain flour

pinch salt

150g cold unsalted butter

½ tsp lemon juice

100ml iced water

If you have a food processor, sift the flour and salt into the bowl and mix. Cut 100g of the butter into rough cubes and add them to the flour mixture. Pulse until it resembles fine breadcrumbs. Cut the rest of the butter into small cubes, add them the blender and pulse briefly to combine. Small lumps of butter should still be obvious in the mixture.

If you are working by hand, sift the flour and salt into a large bowl. Coarsely grate 100g of the butter into the flour mixture. Rub the butter and flour between your fingertips working quickly to keep the mixture as cool as possible. If it starts to feel sticky, chill the mixture for 30 minutes. Then coarsely grate the remaining butter into the mixture and stir. Small lumps or strands of butter should be clearly visible.

Chill the mixture for 30 minutes. Just before you are ready to proceed, stir the lemon juice into the water and pour two-thirds of this into the flour mixture. Blend well with a fork, stirring quickly but gently. Using your fingertips, bring the dough together, adding more water as necessary (you may need to use all of it) until everything is evenly mixed and there are no dry lumps of flour. Bring the mix together into a smooth, supple lump, carefully form it into a flattened ball, wrap in cling film and chill for at least 1 hour before using.

SWEET PASTRY

✳ Makes approx 700g ✳ Preparation time 10 minutes plus 1–2 hours chilling time

This pastry is a combination of two of Mrs Beeton's recipes. The key is to blend the butter well with the flour and, to make this easier, in this recipe you start off with butter that is at room temperature, not chilled, and then beat it until it is light, as you would if you were making a cake. The pastry is then chilled before use, and kneaded lightly to make it supple before rolling it out. This pastry recipe makes enough for a 30cm tart case.

200g unsalted butter, at room temperature

125g icing sugar

1 medium egg, lightly beaten

285g plain flour, plus extra for dusting

In a large bowl, cream the softened butter with a wooden spoon until light. Sift in the icing sugar and combine gently until the two are well mixed.

Add the beaten egg to the bowl, mixing well, then sift in the flour and combine well. When you have obtained a soft dough scrape it into a ball and then flatten it onto a piece of cling film. Cover the dough with the cling film and chill.

After 1–2 hours the dough will be easier to handle. When you are ready to roll out the pastry, remove it from the cling film and knead it lightly to make it supple enough for rolling. Place a sheet of non-stick baking paper on your work surface and scatter it with a little flour. Place the dough on the baking paper and cover with another sheet of baking paper, then roll out between the 2 sheets. This will make it easier to transfer the dough to a pie dish once it has been rolled out.

CUSTARD TART

✳ Serves 8–10 ✳ Preparation time 40 minutes plus 1–2 hours chilling time ✳ Cooking time 1 hour 15 minutes

This recipe, based on Mrs Beeton's baked custard pudding, produces a crisp pastry case filled with silky, smooth custard. Brushing the pastry with egg white after blind baking seals the surface and keeps the pastry crisp while the filling cooks.

1 quantity sweet pastry (see opposite)

unsalted butter, for greasing

plain flour, for dusting

1 egg white, beaten

300ml double cream

300ml whole milk

50g caster sugar

6 large egg yolks

½ tsp nutmeg, finely grated

special equipment

a 20cm loose-based cake tin and some baking beans

Make the pastry, cover and chill for 1–2 hours. When you are ready to start rolling, grease the cake tin, place a large sheet of non-stick baking paper on your work surface and dust it with a little flour. Knead the pastry lightly to make it supple enough to roll, then place it on the baking paper, dust again with flour and put another sheet of baking paper on top. Roll the pastry out between the sheets of paper to a diameter of 30cm. With floured fingers, place the pastry over the tin, pressing it carefully it into the bottom. Trim the edges, cover the lined tin with cling film and chill for 20 minutes.

Preheat the oven to 200°C/gas mark 6. Line the pastry case with non-stick baking paper, fill with baking beans and place in the oven. After 20 minutes turn the oven down to 160°C/gas mark 3 and bake for a further 15–20 minutes, or until the pastry is cooked through. Remove the pastry case from of the oven and take out the paper and beans. If there are any cracks, roll some of the off-cuts in your fingers and use them to fill the gaps, then brush the pastry case with the beaten egg white and return it to the oven for 5 minutes, or until it has browned evenly. Remove from the oven and reduce the temperature to 140°C/gas mark 1.

Place the cream, milk and half the sugar in a saucepan over a low heat and stir occasionally until the sugar dissolves. Meanwhile, in a bowl, whisk the egg yolks with the remaining sugar. Pour the egg yolk mixture into the cream mixture, stir until fully combined, then pass the custard through a sieve and into the pastry case. Sprinkle with the grated nutmeg. Make a loose tent of foil over the tart and bake for 35 minutes, or until the edges are set and the centre is still a little wobbly.

PUFF PASTRY

✳ Makes 2kg ✳ Preparation time 15 minutes plus 20 minutes of rolling over 3 hours

Mrs Beeton gives more than one recipe for 'puff paste' – this classic method is standard and based on the recipe written by Monsieur Ude, one of the foremost French chefs working in London at the beginning of the nineteenth century.

1kg strong plain flour, plus extra for dusting

2 tsp salt

1kg cold unsalted butter

1 tsp lemon juice

500ml cold water

Using a food processor, place all the flour with the salt and 250g of the butter, cut into cubes, into the bowl and pulse until the mixture resembles fine breadcrumbs. Pour this into a large bowl.

Add the lemon juice to the water and add two-thirds of the liquid to the bowl. Blend well with a fork, stirring quickly but gently. Using your fingertips, bring the dough together. Add more water as necessary (you may need all of it) until everything is evenly mixed and there are no dry lumps of flour. Bring the mixture together into a smooth, supple lump. Carefully form it into a flattened ball, wrap in cling film and chill for at least 1 hour before using.

Roll the remaining butter between 2 sheets of non-stick baking paper into an 18cm square that is 2.5cm thick. Lightly flour your work surface, then remove the dough from the fridge and unwrap. Place on the lightly floured surface and cut a deep cross in the dough, cutting about two-thirds of the way through to the work surface. Dust the ball with flour and fold the four segments out into a rough square shape. Dust this lightly with flour and roll it into a square about 28cm across, or large enough to take the block of butter set at a 45° angle.

Using a clean pastry brush, dust the pastry free of flour, place the butter in the centre at a 45° angle to the pastry and fold each corner of the pastry over the butter, pinching the dough together to seal any holes. Turn the flour, and roll the pastry out into a 20 x 60cm rectangle. If the pastry sticks to the work surface dust it with a little more flour as required.

Once you have a rectangle of the right size, brush the pastry to remove any excess flour. Fold the third of the pastry nearest to you over the middle third, then fold in the top third on top of that so that you have a 20 x 20cm square and press, keeping the dough as square and even as you can. Place it on a plate in a cool place or the fridge to rest.

After 15 minutes remove the dough from the fridge and turn it 90° to the right from its original position, so that the top open fold is on your left. Roll out again to 20 x 60cm and repeat the action above. Do this a total of 6 times, allowing the dough to rest in between each fold. After resting it for the last time, roll the pastry into a 30 x 20cm rectangle. Cut this evenly into 4 parts. If you are not using any of the puff pastry straight away, wrap each portion tightly in cling film, then seal in foil and freeze.

APPLE TURNOVERS

✳ Serves 1–2 ✳ Preparation time 5 minutes ✳ Cooking time 15–20 minutes

Here is a handy way of using up off-cuts of puff or flaky shortcrust pastry. You can adjust the quantities of the other ingredients depending on how much leftover pastry you have. Mrs Beeton's fruit turnovers were smaller – great for picnics, but they didn't leave much room for any filling. This larger size gives a better balance of flavours.

plain flour, for dusting

100g puff or flaky shortcrust pastry off-cuts

80g unsweetened apple purée

1 egg white

1 tsp granulated sugar, plus extra for sprinkling

Preheat the oven to 200°C/gas mark 6. Scatter some flour over your work surface. Place the pastry on the surface and roll it out to a 16cm square about 2mm thick.

Spoon the apple purée into the centre then dampen 2 sides of the pastry with a little water. Pull one corner over to form a triangle. Press the edges together firmly to seal. Now whisk the egg white with 1 tsp sugar and brush the mixture all over the surface of the pastry. Sprinkle with a little more granulated sugar, and then carefully lift the turnover onto a baking sheet lined with non-stick baking paper. Place in the oven for 15–20 minutes, or until the turnover is well browned.

Remove from the oven, leave to cool on a wire rack for a few minutes and serve with Jersey cream.

LEMON TART

✱ Serves 8 ✱ Preparation time 30 minutes plus 30 minutes resting time ✱ Cooking time 1 hour 15 minutes

Lemons have always been a popular dessert ingredient, providing a refreshing counterbalance to a rich meal. This classic tart is a perfect example, with the almonds adding a pleasant texture to the zesty filling. The original recipe uses a puff pastry case, but the shortcrust gives a weightier, more refined edge.

½ quantity shortcrust pastry (see page 18)

150g caster sugar

90ml double cream

6 egg yolks

150g butter, melted

40g ground almonds

zest and juice of 2 large lemons

special equipment

a 22cm metal pie or baking dish and some baking beans

First make the pastry and leave it to rest in the fridge for 20 minutes. Then, roll it out on a floured surface to a 27cm round. Place it in the pie dish, leaving the extra pastry hanging over the edge. This technique may seem wasteful, but it will help prevent the pastry shrinking back into the case.

Line the pastry case with a large piece of non-stick baking paper and then fill with baking beans. Leave to rest in a cool place for 10 minutes.

Preheat the oven to 200°C/gas mark 6. Place the pastry case on a baking tray and bake for 35 minutes until the pastry is firm and golden brown. Remove the beans and paper and return the case to the oven for five minutes to bake further and dry slightly.

Remove from the oven and set aside. Reduce the oven to 120°C/gas mark ½.

Now make the filling by beating together the sugar and cream. Then beat in the egg yolks. Beat the melted butter into the mixture, adding it a little at a time.

Fold in the ground almonds along with the lemon juice and zest. Pour the mixture into the pastry case and bake for 40 minutes, or until just set.

Trim the pastry hanging over the rim with a sharp knife and cool to room temperature before serving.

DEEP APPLE PIE

✳ Serves 8 ✳ Preparation time 25 minutes plus 30 minutes chilling time
✳ Cooking time 45 minutes plus 10 minutes cooling time

In the years since Mrs Beeton published her book the Bramley apple has arrived on the scene and now dominates as the cooking apple of choice. Bramleys taste particularly sharp, so if you have access to a different variety you should adjust the quantity of sugar to taste.

1½ quantities flaky shortcrust pastry (see page 19)

1½kg peeled and cored cooking apples

150g plus 1 tbsp caster sugar

1 tbsp lemon juice

1 egg white

2 tbsp granulated sugar, for dredging

special equipment

a deep 22–25cm pie dish and a temperature probe

Make the flaky shortcrust pastry, cover and chill for 30 minutes. Meanwhile, cut the prepared apples into 3mm thick slices and place them in a bowl. Sprinkle over 150g sugar and the lemon juice, stir well and leave to macerate for 5-10 minutes. Preheat the oven to 200°C/gas mark 6.

Roll the pastry into a circle 16cm larger than the diameter of your pie dish. Pile the apple and any juice into dish – it will come high above the rim. Moisten the rim of the pie dish with water. Now cut a 4mm strip from around the outside of the pastry circle and attach it to the rim of the pie dish. Moisten this with a little water and drape the circle of pastry over top to form a lid, sealing well by crimping the edges of the pastry together. Cut away any surplus pastry and reserve.

Cut a 4cm cross in the top of the pie and fold back the four parts to leave a hole for steam to escape. Use any pastry trimmings to make a few leaves as a decoration to surround the hole, but set them aside for the moment.

Beat the egg white with 1 tbsp caster sugar and brush this mixture onto the top of the pie. Now add the leaves as decoration and brush again. Dredge the surface of the pie with the granulated sugar. Place the pie on a baking sheet and set in the centre of the oven for 45 minutes. If the pie browns very quickly, reduce the heat to 160°C/gas mark 3.

Insert a temperature probe into the pie. If it reads 85°C the pie is done. Remove the pie from the oven and leave to cool for 10 minutes then serve it warm with Jersey cream.

PLUM FRANGIPANE TART

✳ Serves 8 ✳ Preparation time 15 minutes plus 1 hour 30 minutes–2 hours 30 minutes chilling time
✳ Cooking time 1 hour 20 minutes

This elegant tart presents a perfect balance of fruit to almond frangipane. Mrs Beeton was a fan of filled pastry tarts, giving many recipes for all manner of nuts and grains. Following her lead, ground rice can be substituted for the almonds used here if you have a nut allergy.

1 quantity sweet pastry
(see page 20)

150g softened unsalted butter

150g caster sugar

3 eggs

½ tsp almond extract

150g ground almonds

scant 2 tbsp plain flour, sifted,
plus extra for dusting

3 tbsp damson or plum jam

600g small purple plums,
stoned and quartered

2 tbsp flaked almonds

special equipment

a 22cm loose-bottomed
tart tin and some baking beans

Make the sweet pastry, cover and chill for 1–2 hours. When it has finished chilling, roll the pastry out to a 30cm circle. Flour your fingers and transfer it to the tart tin, pressing it carefully into the bottom and allowing any extra pastry to hang over the edge. This helps to prevent shrinkage during cooking. Cover the tin loosely with cling film and chill for 20 minutes. Preheat the oven to 200°C/gas mark 6.

Line the chilled pastry case with non-stick baking paper and fill with baking beans. Bake for 20 minutes, then turn the oven down to 160°C/gas mark 3 for a further 15–20 minutes, or until the pastry is cooked through. Once the case is cooked, remove the paper and beans from the tin carefully. If there are any cracks, roll some of the excess pastry trimmings between your fingers to make it pliable and use it to fill the gaps. Return the case to the oven and bake for a further 5 minutes, or until it is evenly brown, then remove it from the oven and set it on a wire rack to cool. Turn the oven up to 180°C/gas mark 4.

Cream the butter with the sugar until light and fluffy then mix in the eggs and almond extract. Fold in the ground almonds and sifted flour and set aside. Now spread the jam evenly over the bottom of the tart case. Pour in the almond mixture, spreading it to the edges, then arrange the quartered plums on top, pushing them in lightly. Sprinkle over the flaked almonds.

Bake for 35–40 minutes, or until the almond mixture is evenly browned and firm. Let stand for a few minutes, then trim any excess pastry from the edges, remove the tart from the tin and leave to cool a little. Serve with clotted cream.

MINCE PIES

✳ Makes 12 deep pies ✳ Preparation time 20 minutes plus 1 hour chilling time ✳ Cooking time 35 minutes

The best thing about these mince pies is that they are made in good-sized tins – muffin tins are just right for the job. The result is that you get more filling than usual. The pastry is midway between the 'puff paste' specified by Mrs Beeton and the more usual shortcrust; the glaze, containing just egg white and sugar, is unusual too. The original recipe doesn't specify how much sugar to use, but here there is lots, to give a really crisp, light crust to the top of the pies.

2 quantities flaky shortcrust pastry (see page 19)

plain flour, for dusting

600g lemon mincemeat (see page 91), made 2–3 months ahead

1 egg white

2 tbsp caster sugar

granulated sugar, for dredging

special equipment

10cm and 5cm round pastry cutters and a deep 12-hole muffin tin

Make the flaky shortcrust pastry and chill it for 30 minutes. Just before the chilling time is over preheat the oven to 200°C/gas mark 6.

Dust your work surface with flour and roll out the pastry on it to a thickness of 3mm. Stamp out 12 rounds 10cm in size and 12 rounds 5cm in size.

Gently press each of the larger disks into one of the 12 holes of the muffin tin, making sure that the edge of the pastry sits slightly proud of the top edge. Divide the mincemeat evenly among the lined muffin-tin holes.

Moisten the edges of the small pastry discs and place each one on top of a pie. Crimp the edges of the pastry together to make a good seal to prevent the mincemeat boiling out. Whisk together the egg white and the caster sugar and brush this mixture over the tops of the pies. Dredge each pie with a little granulated sugar and pierce a hole in centre of each lid with sharp knife or a skewer.

Bake for 10 minutes, or until well browned on top, then reduce the heat to 160°C/gas mark 3. Bake for a further 25 minutes, or until the pies are deep golden brown. Remove the tin from the oven and leave to cool for a few minutes on a wire rack. Then carefully lift the pies from the muffin tin while they are still warm and place on a cooling rack. Eat warm with clotted cream, or store in an airtight tin for up to 3 days.

CAKES

CITRUS POUND CAKE

✳ Serves 6–8 ✳ Preparation time 15 minutes ✳ Cooking time 1 hour

Mrs Beeton's pound cake uses a little almond and citrus to scent the crumb. It is a lovely mixture and quite fine on its own, without frosting or fillings. The simple combination is perfect with a cup of Earl Grey tea.

230g softened unsalted butter, plus extra for greasing

230g caster sugar

4 medium eggs at room temperature

½ tsp almond extract

280g self-raising flour, sifted, plus extra for dusting the tin

70g homemade candied peel (see page 89), cut into small chunks

25g ground almonds

special equipment

a deep cake tin, 20cm round or 17cm square

Preheat the oven to 160°C/gas mark 3. Grease the tin with a little soft butter, then line the base with non-stick baking paper.

In a large bowl, beat the butter until light and soft. Add the caster sugar and cream the two together until the mixture is light and fluffy and the sugar is well incorporated.

Beat the eggs lightly with the almond extract to break them up. Then add this mixture, 2 tbsp at a time, to the butter and sugar mixture, beating well after each addition. When two-thirds of the egg mixture has been incorporated, fold in 1 tbsp sifted flour using a large metal spoon. Fold in the remaining egg mixture and then sift in the remaining flour. Add the cut peel and almonds and fold everything together until all the ingredients are well distributed, but working gently to retain the lightness of the batter.

Pour the batter into the prepared tin and make a small depression in the centre. Place in the centre of the oven for 40 minutes, then reduce the heat to 150°C/gas mark 2 and bake for a further 20–25 minutes, or until the cake is firm to a light touch and a skewer inserted into the middle of the cake comes out cleanly. Or, insert a temperature probe into the centre of the cake. If it registers 95°C the cake is done.

Remove from the oven and cool the cake for 10 minutes in the tin before transferring to a wire cooling rack. When it is completely cool, store it in an airtight container. The lovely flavour of this cake develops further if it is left for 2–3 days before serving.

BARA BRITH

✳ Serves 6-8 ✳ Preparation time 25 minutes plus overnight soaking ✳ Cooking time 50-55 minutes

'Plum breads', like this one, were, and are still, common and the recipes are almost impossible to distinguish from one another. Mrs Beeton gives many variants on this theme. Tea is used to moisten the fruit, and the resulting mixture requires no butter – a cake for hard times, you might think, but one that is delicious and healthy too. You can use any combination of tea and dried fruit, keeping the quantities the same.

400ml freshly made jasmine tea

350g dried dates

80g soft brown sugar

softened butter, for greasing

350g plain white flour

2 tsp baking powder

1 large egg, lightly beaten

25g flaked almonds

special equipment

a 1kg loaf tin

The day before you bake, make the jasmine tea. Place the dates in a large bowl and strain the tea over them. Stir in the sugar, cover and leave overnight.

When you are ready to bake, preheat the oven to 180°C/gas mark 4. Grease the loaf tin with a little soft butter and line the base with a strip of non-stick baking paper.

Sift the flour and baking powder together into a bowl. Mix the beaten egg into the soaked dates then fold them into the flour mixture using a large metal spoon, working quickly but gently.

Transfer the batter to the loaf tin, smooth the surface and then scatter over the flaked almonds.

Set the loaf onto a baking tray and place in the centre of the oven for 50-55 minutes, turning the tin around after 30 minutes. The loaf is ready when a thin skewer pushed into the centre comes out cleanly, or a temperature probe registers 95°C. Remove from the oven and cool in the tin for 10 minutes. Transfer the cake to a wire rack to cool completely before storing in an airtight container. Serve in slices spread with butter and honey.

CARAWAY SEED CAKE

✳ Serves 6–8 ✳ Preparation time 20 minutes ✳ Cooking time 1 hour–1 hour 20 minutes

Mrs Beeton adds a little brandy to her seed cake – a lovely addition, and quite the height of sophistication. Her recipe has been altered here only in that the proportion of flour has been reduced to show just how little you can get away with – the resulting crumb is moist and lighter than the citrus pound cake on page 34.

230g softened unsalted butter, plus extra for greasing

200g caster sugar

3 medium eggs at room temperature

75ml brandy

200g self-raising flour, sifted

1 tsp caraway seeds

pinch ground mace

few gratings of nutmeg

special equipment

a 1kg loaf tin

Preheat the oven to 160°C/gas mark 3. Grease the loaf tin with a little soft butter and line it with non-stick baking paper, leaving an overhang of 2cm on the long sides to help you lift the cake out of the tin when it is baked.

In a large bowl, beat the butter until it is very soft. Add the sugar and cream the two together until light and fluffy.

Lightly beat the eggs and brandy together then add this mixture, 2 tablespoons at a time, to the butter mixture, beating well after each addition. When two-thirds of the egg mixture has been incorporated, fold in 1 tbsp sifted flour using a large metal spoon. Then fold the remaining egg mixture into the batter.

Mix the caraway seeds and the spices with the remaining flour and sift over the batter. Fold it in carefully until there are no lumps. Pour the batter into the prepared loaf tin.

Place in the centre of the oven for 40–50 minutes, then reduce the heat to 150°C/gas mark 2, and bake for a further 25–30 minutes, or until the loaf is a deep golden brown. The loaf is ready when a thin skewer pushed into the centre comes out cleanly, or a temperature probe registers 95°C. If it is not cooked but is browning too much, turn the temperature down to 130°C/gas mark 1/2 and cover the top of the loaf with a piece of foil. Test again after 10 minutes. When it is done remove from the oven and cool in the tin for 10 minutes. Transfer the cake to a wire rack to cool completely before storing in an airtight container.

DARK CHOCOLATE CAKE

✻ Serves 6–8 ✻ Preparation time 15 minutes ✻ Cooking time 20 minutes

A variation on Mrs Beeton's chocolate soufflé recipe, this cake uses whole rather than separated eggs, and includes butter. Those two elements combine to give a fudgy texture that is fantastic when served just warm, with whipped cream on the side.

150g slightly salted butter, plus extra for greasing

40g cocoa powder, plus extra for dusting

200g plain dark chocolate (65–70% cocoa solids)

5 medium eggs at room temperature

1 egg yolk at room temperature

70g soft brown sugar

150g caster sugar

3 tbsp brandy

90g plain flour

special equipment

a deep 23cm round spring-form cake tin and a large heatproof bowl

Preheat the oven to 160°C/gas mark 3. Grease the cake tin with a little soft butter, then pour some cocoa powder into the tin, rolling it around to coat the inside and tipping out any excess. Then line the base with non-stick baking paper.

Place the butter and chocolate in a large heatproof bowl and set it over a pan of barely simmering water on a low heat. Do not allow the bottom of the bowl to touch the water. Leave the chocolate to melt without stirring.

Place the eggs, egg yolk and sugars in the bowl of an electric mixer. Beat at high speed for 10–15 minutes, or until light and creamy, then add the brandy and beat until combined.

Sieve the cocoa and flour together. Working quickly but gently, first fold the chocolate and butter mixture into the egg mix using a large metal spoon, and when this is evenly combined, fold in the cocoa and flour, ensuring that there are no lumps or bits of dry flour.

Pour the batter into the prepared tin and bake for 20 minutes. Once cooked, allow the cake to cool in the tin, then carefully remove the sides of the tin and slice with a sharp knife dipped in hot water.

The cake will remain deliciously moist and fudgy in the middle. Serve it at room temperature with some whipped cream and fresh raspberries on the side.

DARK GINGERBREAD

✳ Serves 6-8 ✳ Preparation time 20 minutes ✳ Cooking time 45 minutes

This is a classic gingerbread, dark and moist. I have reduced the quantity of flour from the original recipe to make a lighter cake and added some fresh root ginger to add spice and aroma. It can be iced or left plain and will keep for a week or more, after which it is best sliced and eaten spread with a little salted butter.

115g unsalted butter or lard, plus extra for greasing

225g black treacle

225g golden syrup

115g brown sugar, sieved if lumpy

50g finely grated fresh root ginger

375g plain flour

4 tsp ground ginger

4 tsp cinnamon

4 tsp mixed spice

pinch salt

1 tsp bicarbonate of soda

¼ pint milk

3 medium eggs

for the icing

150g icing sugar

2 tbsp ginger wine or syrup

2 lobes of stem ginger in syrup, drained and finely chopped, to decorate

special equipment

a 23cm square baking tin

Preheat the oven to 180°C/gas mark 4. Grease the baking tin and line the base with non-stick baking paper.

Place the treacle, syrup, sugar and butter or lard in a medium-sized saucepan over a low heat and warm until the fat has just melted. Remove from the heat and stir in the grated root ginger.

Sift the flour, spices, salt and bicarbonate of soda together into a large bowl until well blended then add the melted ingredients stirring well to combine. Lightly beat the milk and eggs together and then pour them into treacle and flour mixture and stir to form a smooth, loose batter.

Pour the batter into the prepared tin and bake in the centre of the oven for 45 minutes, or until the gingerbread is evenly cooked and firm to the touch. Leave to cool in the tin on a wire rack for 15 minutes.

Make the icing by placing the icing sugar in a bowl and adding the ginger wine or syrup and mixing until you have a thick, pouring consistency. Turn the cooled gingerbread out of the tin, drizzle over the icing and sprinkle with the chopped ginger. Leave the icing to dry for 2–3 hours before serving. You can also transfer the gingerbread to an airtight container, but eat within 1 week of making.

LEMON SPONGE

✳ Serves 10 ✳ Preparation time 20 minutes ✳ Cooking time 40 minutes

This versatile cake is especially nice served sliced with lemon curd (see page 90) and whipped cream. It can also be used, sliced and layered, in a trifle.

25g unsalted butter, melted, plus a little extra for greasing

4 medium eggs

115g caster sugar

1 tbsp orange flower water

finely grated zest of ½ lemon

115g plain flour, sifted

special equipment

a deep 20cm round cake tin

Preheat the oven to 180°C/gas mark 4. Grease the cake tin with a little soft butter, then line the base with non-stick baking paper.

Using an electric mixer, whisk the eggs for a minute then add the sugar and orange flower water. Beat at high speed for 10–15 minutes until the mixture is light and mousse-like.

Working quickly but gently, fold in the lemon zest and flour, and then the melted butter. Make sure all of the ingredients are well incorporated and there are no lumps.

Pour the batter into the prepared tin and place in the centre of the oven. After 25 minutes turn the oven down to 160°C/gas mark 3 for a further 15 minutes. The cake is cooked when it is evenly browned all over or firm to a light touch and a skewer inserted into the middle of the cake comes out cleanly. Or, insert a temperature probe into the centre of the cake. If it registers 95°C the cake is done.

HONEY MADELEINES

✳ Makes about 20 ✳ Preparation time 20 minutes plus 40 minutes resting time ✳ Cooking time 10 minutes

Mrs Beeton uses 'honey to taste' in her honey cake, which is unusually vague for her. Here, a more precise quantity is given, but honey can also be used in place of part of the sugar if you prefer. Based on Mrs Beeton's small sponge cakes, these madeleines have the added benefit of cooking quickly, overcoming the tendency of honey to brown too quickly in the oven.

120g unsalted butter, plus a little extra for greasing

50g English honey

3 medium eggs at room temperature

100g caster sugar

100g self-raising flour, plus extra for dusting the tins

25g ground almonds

special equipment

2 x 10-hole madeleine tins

Place the butter in a small pan to melt over a medium-high heat. Allow it to cook until it begins to brown lightly. As soon as it turns a light caramel colour, remove it from the heat and stir in the honey to halt the cooking process then set it aside to cool slightly.

Meanwhile place the eggs and sugar in a large bowl and whisk with an electric mixer until light and fluffy. This will take approximately 10–15 minutes.

Sift the flour and ground almonds together and fold into the mixture using a large metal spoon or a spatula. Then fold in the cooled butter and honey mixture until fully incorporated.

Cover and place in the fridge for 30 minutes.

Grease the madeleine tins with butter and dust them lightly with plain flour.

When the batter has chilled, divide it between the moulds. Let it rest for 10 minutes at room temperature while you preheat the oven to 160°C/gas mark 3.

Bake for 10 minutes, or until light golden and springy to the touch. Allow them to cool for 2–3 minutes in the tin (this will make them easier to remove) and then cool on a wire rack. Store in an airtight tin for up to 4 days.

TEATIME
TREATS

Afternoon Tea

Afternoon tea was beginning to be a popular institution in Mrs Beeton's time and today it is hugely popular. Served at home, it provides the perfect excuse to get out your best china and spend an unhurried hour or two indulging in elaborate rituals and the exquisite delights of hot buttered scones, fancy pastries, dainty little cucumber sandwiches and, of course, a refreshing cuppa.

Hot drinks

What we know as **tea** derives from an evergreen plant related to the camellia. The new shoots of the tea bush are highly prized and generally make the finest tea. Once picked, the leaves are dried immediately to produce green tea, or fermented until dark to make black tea. The flavour and character of each tea variety and region varies enormously, so try as many as you can until you find one you love. The best-quality tea is sold in leaf form from specialist shops. It does not keep forever so only buy 100–200g at a time. To keep it fresh, seal in an airtight container in a cool, dark place.

To make tea, boil plenty of fresh water in a kettle. Pour a little of this into the teapot and swirl it around to warm the pot, while the rest of the water cools down in the kettle for a minute or so. Pour away the water from the teapot and add the tea, using one level teaspoon of loose-leaf tea per cup, plus one teaspoon 'for the pot'. If you are using bags, use one per person. Pour the water – about 200ml per cup – over the tea, put the lid on the pot and leave to steep. For a light-coloured tea, leave for one and a half minutes. If you prefer your tea stronger steep it for a maximum of five minutes.

The two major varieties of **coffee** that are grown today are *Coffea arabica* and *Coffea canephora* (also known as Robusta). The coffee bean is covered with a fleshy coat, inside which is a pale green bean. It is possible to buy raw coffee beans to roast at home, but most of us buy beans ready-roasted to varying degrees – the darker the roast, the more intense the flavour. Many of the flavour compounds in coffee are volatile, so it is important to buy your coffee often and in small quantities from a dealer who roasts their beans regularly. Alternatively, buy it in vacuum packs and, once opened, chill or freeze in an airtight container to keep the coffee fresher for longer.

To make coffee, use one dessertspoon (7g) per cup plus one for the pot. Leave the kettle to stand for a few minutes after boiling, so that the water drops a few degrees in temperature (the ideal temperature for brewing coffee is 94°C), and then pour the water over the coffee – use about 200ml per cup for a medium-strength brew. Stir, then leave to brew for two or three minutes before serving.

For those craving something sweeter, a cup of **drinking chocolate** is a quick and indulgent treat (see page 63) – perfect for breakfast, afternoon tea, or anytime of the day or night.

PLAIN SCONES

✳ Makes 20 small scones ✳ Preparation time 10 minutes ✳ Cooking time 10-12 minutes

Little cakes raised with baking powder have always been popular and are quick to make. Mrs Beeton gives two recipes that are similar to our modern scone, breakfast cakes and soda buns, both of which have a neutral dough that is excellent when buttered or eaten with jam. She uses just a little sugar or none at all, substituting currants instead for sweetness. Should you want to try this, add 115g of currants in the place of the sugar. Split the scones when cool and fill with clotted cream and jam, or spread with butter and heather honey.

450g self-raising flour, plus extra for dusting

115g cold unsalted butter, diced

pinch salt

60g caster sugar

175ml milk

1 tbsp lemon juice

special equipment

a 4–5cm round pastry cutter

Preheat the oven to 200°C/gas mark 6.

Place the flour, butter, salt and sugar into a food processor and blend until the mixture is very fine and lump-free. Pour the mixture onto a work surface and make a well in the centre. Stir the milk and lemon juice together in a bowl or jug, then pour into the well in the dry ingredients.

Using a large fork, work steadily out from the centre to mix the flour quickly and gently into the liquid until you have an even mixture with no wet or dry patches. Scrape up any dough sticking to the work surface using a spatula and incorporate this into the mix. Do not knead the mixture. Simply pinch it together with your fingertips until it forms a ball. If it seems a little dry, add a splash more milk.

Scatter some flour over your work surface, rolling pin and 2 baking trays. Gently roll the dough out to a thickness of 3cm on the floured work surface. Dip your cutter into some flour and then stamp out a round in the dough sheet and place it on the baking tray. Dipping your cutter in flour between each cut will ensure the scones rise evenly.

When you have used all the dough, dust the scones lightly with flour. Bake in the centre of the oven for 10–12 minutes, or until well risen and a light golden-brown. The scones are ready when they sound hollow when tapped on the bottom. Transfer the scones to a wire rack until completely cool, then store in an airtight tin or freeze.

ALMOND MACAROONS

✳ Makes 50–60 shells ✳ Preparation time 15 minutes plus 20 minutes resting time ✳ Cooking time 15 minutes

Although Mrs Beeton said of macaroons that it was 'almost or quite as economical to purchase such articles as these at a good confectioner's', that is certainly not the case today – so do try this recipe. You will get a smoother, glossier result if your almonds are ground as finely as possible and you dry them in a warm place for a couple of hours before using them. These macaroons are especially good spread with fresh raspberry jam.

140g ground almonds

200g icing sugar

seeds scraped from
2 vanilla pods

4 medium egg whites

pinch cream of tartar

60g caster sugar

for the filling

raspberry jam (see page 84),
to sandwich

special equipment

a piping bag fitted with a
round nozzle

Before you begin, spread the ground almonds onto a baking sheet and leave them to dry in a warm place for 2 hours. Once they have dried, preheat oven to 140°C/gas mark 1. Line 2 baking sheets with non-stick baking paper.

Place the ground almonds, icing sugar and vanilla seeds into a food processor and blitz for 20 seconds to make the almonds as fine as possible and to combine them thoroughly with the sugar. Sift the mixture into a bowl.

Place the egg whites into the bowl of an electric mixer with the cream of tartar and beat on a medium speed until they become light and foamy. Increase the speed and add the caster sugar, a little at a time, until the sugar is fully incorporated and the mixture forms soft peaks.

Sift the almond mixture, one-third at a time, onto the egg whites, folding together after each addition. Continue to fold until the mixture becomes smooth and glossy, then spoon into a piping bag fitted with a round nozzle and pipe rounds 2–3cm in diameter onto the prepared baking sheets, leaving 3cm between the rounds. Leave to rest for 20 minutes to allow a skin to form on top of the macaroons, then bake for 15 minutes until set. Transfer the macaroons to a wire rack and leave to cool completely.

Use the jam to sandwich the macaroons together in pairs, and leave for 1 hour to allow the jam to soak in. Store in an airtight container for up to 1 week or, better yet, eat the next day.

SUNDERLAND GINGERNUTS

✳ Makes 25 biscuits ✳ Preparation time 15 minutes ✳ Cooking time 15–20 minutes

Mrs Beeton's spice mixture for these biscuits is lovely, with a little coriander being added for greater depth of flavour – an addition that is rarely seen today. The quantity of flour has been reduced to give a lighter, crisper result.

100g softened unsalted butter

75g caster sugar

20g black treacle or molasses

120g golden syrup

1½ tsp ground ginger

½ tsp ground allspice

½ tsp ground coriander

¾ tsp bicarbonate of soda

220g self-raising flour

100g demerara sugar

Preheat the oven to 180°C/gas mark 4. Line 2 baking sheets with non-stick baking paper.

Cream the butter and sugar in a large bowl until light and fluffy. Add the treacle or molasses and the syrup and beat the mixture until combined. In another bowl, sift all the ground spices, the bicarbonate of soda and the flour together then add to the butter mixture. Mix with your fingertips into an even dough that is free of lumps.

Pour the demerara sugar evenly on to a large flat dish. Now take a lump of dough about the size of a walnut, shape it into a ball and roll it in the demerara sugar, repeating with all the dough until the mixture is used up. Arrange the balls at least 4cm apart on the prepared baking sheets and flatten each one slightly using a fork. Bake for 5 minutes then turn the heat down to 160°C/gas mark 3 for a further 10–15 minutes.

The biscuits will rise and then fall. Once the surface of the biscuits cracks and they are firm and a dark golden brown all over remove them from the oven and leave them to cool for 10 minutes. Transfer the biscuits to a wire rack to cool completely and then store in an airtight container.

ENGLISH MUFFINS

✳ Makes 10 muffins ✳ Preparation time 10 minutes mixing plus 2 hours rising time
✳ Cooking time 20–30 minutes

Mrs Beeton toasted her muffins, not too dark, and piled them high, well buttered to melt together, just as she did with her toast. They are straightforward to make and delicious.

230ml milk

5g dried yeast

400g strong white bread flour, plus extra for dusting

100g plain white flour

10g salt

15g caster sugar

20g melted butter, plus a little extra for greasing

fine semolina, for dusting

special equipment

10 x 10cm muffin or poaching rings, a pastry cutter of the same size, a non-stick griddle or heavy-bottomed frying pan and a temperature probe

Pour the milk and 150ml water into a small pan and warm to 40°C over a low heat, then pour into a large bowl. Whisk in the yeast, then sift in 200g strong white bread flour, stirring until smooth. Cover the bowl with a clean, damp tea towel and leave in a warm place for 1 hour, or until doubled in volume.

Sift the remaining ingredients, except the butter and the semolina, into the bowl. Mix thoroughly with your hands, making sure no bits of dry flour are left. Add the melted butter and mix well. Continue to knead and squeeze in the bowl for 5 minutes, until the dough feels smooth and elastic but not hard, then cover the bowl again and leave in a warm place for 30 minutes, or until almost doubled in volume. Meanwhile, dust 2 baking sheets with semolina. Grease 10 muffin or poaching rings and arrange them on the baking sheets.

Flour your work surface, set the dough onto it and gently press it out to a thickness of 2cm, using your hands. Use the pastry cutter to stamp out rounds, placing each one in a muffin ring as you go and re-rolling the dough if necessary. Cover the baking sheets with a clean, dry tea towel and leave the muffins to rise in a warm place until the dough reaches the top of the rings and is beginning to dome.

Heat the frying pan over a medium-high heat. Using a palette knife or spatula, carefully lift each muffin, still in the ring, and place it into the pan. Depending on its size, you may be able to cook 4–5 muffins at once. Cook for 4 minutes on each side, or until they sound hollow when tapped. Place the muffins on a wire rack, remove the rings and leave to cool while you cook the next batch. Store in an airtight tin for up to 2 days.

SCOTCH PANCAKES

✻ Makes 20 pancakes ✻ Preparation time 5 minutes ✻ Cooking time 15–20 minutes

Flat, griddle cakes of this type have been cooked for centuries on top of the stove or
hearth, and they remain popular in Scotland – hence the name. This recipe is based on
Mrs Beeton's nice breakfast cakes, but does not require the oven, and is therefore more
economical. The syrup helps the pancakes brown evenly and keeps their crumb tender.
They are excellent served with crisp bacon and marmalade.

225g self-raising flour

pinch salt

1½ tbsp golden syrup,
warmed

1 tbsp sunflower oil, plus
extra for oiling

2 medium eggs at room temperature

180ml whole or semi-
skimmed milk

special equipment

a non-stick griddle

Sift the flour and salt into a bowl and make a well in the
centre. In another bowl or large jug, whisk the warmed
syrup, oil, eggs and milk together. Pour the milk mixture
into the flour mixture and whisk to combine. Be careful
not to over-mix otherwise the cooked pancakes will not be
tender. Do not worry if there are a few tiny lumps of flour.

The consistency by now should be that of very thick double
cream. If the batter seems a little thick, add some extra milk.

Heat the griddle or a heavy-bottomed frying pan to
medium-high and wipe with a little sunflower oil. Drop a
dessertspoonful of the batter onto the griddle, spreading it
slightly with the back of the spoon to make a round about
7.5cm in diameter. Repeat with another 4, so that you have 5
cooking at a time.

After about 1–2 minutes, or when a deep golden-brown skin
has formed on the underside, flip the pancakes over using a
spatula and cook for another 1–2 minutes until a skin forms
underneath and the pancake feels springy to the touch.

Transfer to a warmed plate and cover with a clean tea towel.
Wipe the griddle between batches to remove any debris and
repeat with remaining batter until you have used it all up.

WELSH CAKES

✳ Makes 15 cakes ✳ Preparation time 10 minutes ✳ Cooking time 30–35 minutes

Mrs Beeton uses dripping or lard in many of her small cakes. The lard gives a 'short' dough that is best eaten warm with salted butter. Bilberry jam, common still in upland areas, makes the perfect accompaniment. Visit any Welsh market town and you will be able to buy these wonderful little cakes. They are often served with jam made from bilberries, which can be found growing on the upland heaths of Wales in the autumn.

150g self-raising flour, plus extra for dusting

pinch salt

50g caster sugar

½ tsp mixed spice

50g lard

30g currants

30g sultanas

1 egg

2 tbsp milk

special equipment

a non-stick griddle or frying pan and a 6.5cm round pastry cutter

Place flour, salt, sugar, mixed spice and lard in a food processor. Blend for 2 minutes or until evenly mixed.

Transfer to a bowl and stir in the currants and sultanas. In another bowl, beat the egg and milk together and pour them into the flour mixture. Using a large fork, quickly but gently fold everything together.

Scatter some flour on your work surface and dust your fingers with flour. Place the mixture on to the floured surface and bring it together into a ball using your hands. Scatter some flour on your rolling pin and roll the dough out to a thickness of 4mm. Stamp 15 rounds out of the dough using the cutter.

Preheat the griddle or frying pan on a medium–low heat then add the cakes a few at a time. Cook the cakes for 4–5 minutes, or until the undersides are golden brown, then cook the other side. Transfer the finished cakes to a wire rack to cool while you cook the rest. Serve with unsalted butter and either jam or honey. These cakes can be stored in an airtight tin for up to 4 days or frozen for up to 1 month.

ECCLES CAKES

✳ Makes 6-8 large cakes ✳ Prep time 10 minutes ✳ Cooking time 35 minutes

Mrs Beeton's mince pies were made with puff pastry rather than the shortcrust that is more often used today, giving a result that is strongly reminiscent of Eccles cakes. As there is already a faithfully rendered Mrs Beeton mince pie recipe on page 30, her mincemeat filling has been replaced here with a simple mixture of currants and lemon zest to give a true Eccles cake. Although Mrs Beeton may not have approved, these are delicious served with some good Cheshire or Lancashire cheese. If you've got some homemade puff pastry (see pages 22–23) in the freezer, thaw out 500g and use it here.

500g currants

125g unsalted butter

125g caster sugar, plus an extra pinch

zest of 2 lemons

plain flour, for dusting

500g puff pastry (see pages 218–219)

1 egg white, beaten

pinch caster sugar

granulated sugar, for dredging

special equipment

a 10–12cm round pastry cutter

Preheat the oven to 200°C/gas mark 6 and line a baking sheet with non-stick baking paper. Place the currants, butter, caster sugar and lemon zest in a small pan over a low heat. Cook, stirring, for 5 minutes then remove from the heat and leave to cool.

Scatter some flour onto your work surface and roll the puff pastry out to a 3-4mm thick sheet. Cut out 6-8 rounds using a cutter (or a small saucer). Re-roll any trimmings if you need to.

Divide the filling between the circles and dampen the edges of the pastry with a little water. Bring the edges together, making sure the filling is covered, and pinch hard, twisting off any excess. Turn the balls over, flattening them slightly, keeping their shape circular. Place on the prepared baking sheet.

Mix the beaten egg white with a pinch of caster sugar and brush the mixture over the cakes, then sprinkle them heavily with granulated sugar. Finally, cut a 2cm slit in the top of each.

Bake for 20 minutes, or until the cakes are brown and crispy then turn the heat down to 140°C/gas mark 1 for a further 15 minutes. The cakes are ready when the undersides are browned and firm. Remove to a cooling rack. Once the cakes are completely cold, they can be stored in an airtight tin for up to 3 days.

RICH FRUIT CAKE

✳ Serves 10-12 ✳ Preparation time 1 hour plus overnight soaking ✳ Cooking time 2 hours 30 minutes–3 hours

Mrs Beeton provided several recipes for fruit cakes, offering a different one for each occasion – among them a treacle-rich Christmas cake and a 'Bride or Christening' cake, both of which are quite different from the fruit cakes we are used to eating today. This basic recipe can be spiced or altered to suit your own taste. It is fruit-heavy and delicious and like most rich fruit cakes, it benefits from being made a month or so before you intend to use it.

700g mixed dried fruit
(raisins, sultanas and currants)

50g homemade candied peel,
chopped (see page 89)

50g glacé cherries, halved

115g flaked almonds

60ml each brandy and
sweet sherry

finely grated zest of 1 lemon

160g softened unsalted butter, plus
extra for greasing

160g soft brown sugar

1 tbsp black treacle or
molasses

3 medium eggs

3 tbsp milk

pinch salt

½ tsp ground mace

½ tsp freshly grated nutmeg

½ tsp mixed spice

200g sifted plain flour

special equipment

a deep 17cm round cake tin

Combine the dried fruit, peel, cherries, almonds, sherry and brandy in a large bowl. Stir, cover and leave overnight.

The next day, add the lemon zest to the fruit and stir well. Preheat the oven to 140°C/gas mark 1. Line a baking tray with a double layer of foil. Grease the tin and line the base and sides with non-stick baking paper. Secure a sheet of newspaper around the outside of the tin with a paperclip.

In a large bowl, cream together the butter and sugar until light and fluffy. Beat in the treacle or molasses. Beat the eggs and milk together and add to the butter mixture in 3-4 batches, beating well between each addition. Now sift together the salt, spices and flour and fold them into the mixture until just combined. Add the fruit and stir to distribute it evenly through the batter, then transfer the batter to the tin. Make a shallow depression in the middle.

Place the tin on the baking tray and cover securely with a sheet of foil. Bake in the centre of the oven for 2½ hours, turning every 30 minutes. Check whether the cake is cooked by inserting a skewer into the middle. If it comes out clean, the cake is done. If not, reduce the oven temperature to 130°C/gas mark ½ and retest after 30 minutes.

Cool overnight in the tin, then carefully turn it out, leaving the baking paper in place, and store in an airtight container for a month or so before using. If you like, you can feed it every week for 3-4 weeks with 2-3 tbsp brandy. Simply drizzle the brandy onto the surface and let it soak in.

VICTORIA SANDWICH CAKE

✳ Serves 8 ✳ Preparation time 15 minutes ✳ Cooking time 25–30 minutes

In 1861 the Victoria sandwich (which supposedly pays tribute to Queen Victoria's love of afternoon tea) had not yet been named. Instead Mrs Beeton included a recipe for Savoy cake. This similarly plain sponge was baked in a tall, elaborate mould – and in order to create the volume necessary for all that cake, Mrs Beeton used seven eggs, whisking the whites and yolks separately before folding them back together. In spite of all this grandeur, she recommended simply slicing the cake and spreading it with jam, 'which converts it into sandwiches'. Today, the cake is sandwiched together with jam before serving. As we use standard tins, fewer eggs are required and there is no need to separate them. This cake can be eaten fresh or made a couple of days in advance to allow the jam to soak in.

eggs weighing 220–240g in total – approx 4 medium eggs

220–240g softened unsalted butter, plus extra for greasing

220–240g caster sugar, plus extra for dusting

220–240g self-raising flour

½ tsp vanilla extract

3–4 tbsp sharp raspberry jam

special equipment

2 x 20cm loose-bottomed cake tins

Preheat the oven to 160°C/gas mark 3. Grease the cake tins and line the bases with non-stick baking paper.

Crack the eggs into a bowl on a scale, then measure out the butter, sugar and flour to the same weight (220–240g). In a large mixing bowl, beat the butter until it is light and fluffy. Add the caster sugar and cream the two together well. Lightly beat the vanilla into the eggs, then add the eggs 2 tbsp at a time to the butter mixture, beating well at each addition to prevent the mixture separating. When two-thirds of the egg has been incorporated, sift in 1 tbsp flour and stir. Add the remaining egg mix, then sift in the remaining flour and fold it with a large metal spoon until the mixture is free of lumps.

Split the batter between the tins, making a small indent in the middle of each. Bake in the centre of the oven for 25–30 minutes, or until risen, evenly browned and firm to the touch. Remove from the oven and run a knife round the inside edge of each tin. Cool the cakes for 10 minutes in the tins, then carefully turn them out onto a wire rack, peel away the baking paper and leave to cool completely.

Place one cake top-side down onto a serving plate. Spread the bottom evenly with the jam, then carefully set the other cake (top-side up) on top. Sprinkle with the caster sugar.

DRINKING CHOCOLATE

✻ Makes 300ml or 1 serving ✻ Preparation time 1 minute ✻ Cooking time 5 minutes

Mrs Beeton used half water and half milk for her hot chocolate, but this recipe uses all milk for a richer result and gives the option of adding honey for an even more indulgent drink. The freshly grated chocolate gives a luxurious, silky texture, but you can use cocoa powder for a lighter result if you prefer.

260ml semi-skimmed milk

1 tsp English honey or ½ tsp caster sugar, to taste

60g dark chocolate, (65–75% cocoa solids), grated, or 2 tsp cocoa powder

Place the milk in a saucepan over a medium heat. Add the honey or sugar and bring to a simmer.

Whisk the grated chocolate or the cocoa powder into the hot milk until the chocolate has melted and the mixture is smooth. Simmer for 1 minute, add more honey or sugar to taste and serve.

'As soon as the drawing-room bell rings for tea, the footman enters with the tray, which has been previously prepared; hands the tray round to the company, with cream and sugar, the tea and coffee being generally poured out, while another attendant hands [round] cakes, toast, biscuits … or such other eatables as may be required, removing the whole in the same manner when tea is over.'

Beeton's Book of Household Management

BREAD &
SWEET BUNS

MALTED SODA BREAD

✳ Makes 2 large loaves ✳ Preparation time 20 minutes ✳ Cooking time 50 minutes

Mrs Beeton gives a recipe for soda bread that uses just 'flour' – and you can of course use whatever type you like. This updated recipe uses malted flour, which adds a delicious flavour. It is wonderful with smoked salmon or cheese and lovely toasted with bacon and marmalade the next day. Leavened with bicarbonate of soda, rather than yeast, it can be made from scratch in just over an hour.

375g plain flour

375g malted flour

150g porridge oats, plus extra for sprinkling

2 tsp bicarbonate of soda

1½ tsp salt

25g caster sugar

350ml milk

475g plain yoghurt

50g black treacle or molasses, warmed gently in a small pan

75g butter, melted, plus extra for greasing

special equipment

2 x 1kg loaf tins

Preheat the oven to 200°C/gas mark 6. Grease the loaf tins and line each with a piece of non-stick baking paper, leaving a slight overhang along the long sides of each tin. This will help the bread rise evenly.

Sift all the dry ingredients into a large bowl, mix them together and make a well in the centre. In another bowl, combine the milk, yoghurt, treacle or molasses and the melted butter, mixing well so there are no lumps. Working quickly, add this to the dry ingredients and combine with a large fork to form a soft, stretchy dough.

Divide the dough equally between the two tins, pressing the batter gently into the corners of the tins. Wet your fingers and gently smooth the surface of the mixture.

Sprinkle the top of the loaves with a few oats and bake in the centre of the oven for 20 minutes. Then turn the oven down to 180°C/gas mark 4 and bake for a further 30 minutes, or until the loaves have browned well and have risen evenly. Test the bread to see if it is ready by tipping it from the tin and knocking the bottom of the loaf. If it sounds hollow, the bread should be ready. Or, insert a temperature probe into the centre of each loaf. If it registers 95°C the loaf is done.

Remove the loaves from the tins and transfer to a wire rack to cool for 20 minutes before cutting. Serve still slightly warm or store in an airtight container and eat within 3 days.

WHOLEMEAL BREAD

✳ Makes 2 large loaves ✳ Preparation time 40 minutes plus 4 hours rising and resting time
✳ Cooking time 40–50 minutes

The flours that are available to us today vary enormously from those Mrs Beeton used. The change is partly due to improvements in milling technology, which have made flour whiter and whiter, and partly thanks to the fact that we now appreciate the benefits of wholemeal flour when for centuries it was considered coarse and fit only for the poor.

550ml water

620g strong wholemeal flour

150g strong white flour, plus extra for dusting

7g dried yeast

15g salt

70g unsalted butter, melted

special equipment

2 x 1kg loaf tins and a temperature probe

Warm the water to 30°C in a saucepan over a low heat, then pour it into a large bowl and add all the other ingredients except the butter. Mix with your hands until everything is evenly combined, then add the butter and squeeze it into the dough using your fingers. The dough will feel sticky.

Leave the dough to rest in a warm place for 20 minutes covered with a damp tea towel. Then scatter some flour over your work surface and place the dough on it. Knead the dough for 2–3 minutes then cover it and leave it to rest for 5 minutes. Repeat, kneading for 2–3 minutes and resting for 5 until the dough is elastic and soft but not sticky. Place the kneaded dough in a bowl, cover with a clean, damp tea towel and leave in a warm place for 1–1½ hours, or until doubled in volume. Towards the end of the rising time grease the 2 loaf tins.

On a floured work surface, divide the dough in 2. Gently shape each half into a round, cover with a clean, dry tea towel and leave to rest for 5 minutes, then flatten each round, roll into a cylinder and place in a prepared tin. Put the tins on a baking sheet, cover with a clean towel and leave in a warm place for 45 minutes, or until the loaves are rising proud of the tins. Preheat the oven to 220°C/gas mark 7.

Slash the tops of the loaves 3–4 times diagonally, then place them in the oven. After 10 minutes turn the oven down to 180°C/gas mark 4. Bake for 30–40 minutes more, or until the loaves are dark golden brown. Remove the loaves from the tins and cool on a wire rack. Store in an airtight tin for up to 2 days.

ENRICHED DOUGH FOR SWEET BUNS

✳ Preparation time 20 minutes plus 1–1 ¼ hours rising and resting time

The following four recipes give only a small indication of the range of English yeasted cakes and buns. Historically, yeasted sweet cakes were far more common than they are now – we tend to use eggs to leaven cakes today, as they are widely available year round (which they weren't historically) and relatively inexpensive. These recipes often have a very regional basis, but they can all be made from the same basic dough, with only minor adjustments. The basic dough recipe is given here.

80ml water

75ml whole milk

5g dried yeast

220g strong white flour

2 egg yolks

55g plain white flour, plus extra for dusting

¾ tsp salt

30g caster sugar

30g butter, melted

special equipment

a temperature probe

First, heat the water and milk in a small saucepan over a low heat until the mixture is tepid, not more than 30°C.

In a large bowl, whisk this mixture with the yeast and 130g of the strong flour until the ingredients combine into a smooth batter. Cover and leave in warm place for 45 minutes to an hour, or until doubled in size.

Beat the egg yolks into the batter then combine the remaining flour, salt and sugar together and add to the batter. Use your hands to bring all the ingredients together and knead for 2 minutes. Next add the melted butter a little at a time and continue to mix until all the butter is incorporated. Rest the dough, covered with a damp tea towel, in a warm place for 15 minutes then proceed as advised for each recipe.

HOT CROSS BUNS

✳ Makes 8 large buns ✳ Preparation time 3 hours including rising and resting time
✳ Cooking time 15–20 minutes

1 quantity enriched dough (see page 69) but made with 7g dried yeast and an extra 25g butter

30g raisins

50g chopped mixed peel

25g sultanas

1 tsp mixed spice

1 tsp ground cinnamon

for the cross paste

100g plain flour

20g caster sugar

for the glaze

50g apricot jam (see page 87)

1 tbsp caster sugar

special equipment

a piping bag fitted with a small round nozzle

Make the dough as directed, with a little extra yeast, then add the additional 25g melted butter at the end.

After 15 minutes resting, uncover the dough and add the dried fruit and spices. Blend them in by breaking up the dough and kneading in the ingredients. When fully combined, turn the dough out onto a lightly floured work surface and knead for 10 minutes, or until it feels soft and smooth and the ingredients are evenly distributed. The dough should feel slightly tacky but not sticky. Add a little flour as you knead if it is too sticky. Shape the dough into a round and place it in a lightly oiled bowl. Cover with a clean, dry tea towel and leave to rise in a warm place for 1–1½ hours, or until almost doubled in size.

Line a baking tray with non-stick baking paper. Flour your work surface and place the dough onto it. Divide the dough evenly into 8 pieces, shape each one into a round ball and arrange them on the baking tray, spaced about 2cm apart and covered loosely with cling film. Leave in a warm place for 30 minutes, or until almost doubled in size.

Meanwhile, preheat the oven to 180°C/gas mark 4 and make the cross paste. Sift the flour and sugar into a bowl, add 75ml water and mix to a thick, smooth paste. Using a piping bag fitted with a small round nozzle, pipe a cross onto each bun. Bake for 15–20 minutes, or until the buns are golden brown. While the buns are baking make the glaze. Place a small pan over a medium heat. Add the apricot jam, caster sugar and 50ml water. Heat until simmering, then cook until the sugar and jam have dissolved and the mix has reduced by one-third.

Paint the glaze onto the buns as they come out of the oven. Serve immediately, split open and spread with salted butter, or store in an airtight tin for up to 3 days. or in the freezer for up to 1 month.

CHELSEA BUNS

✳ Makes 7 ✳ Preparation time 3 hours including rising time ✳ Cooking time 20 minutes

1 quantity enriched dough
(see page 69)

100g softened unsalted butter,
plus a little extra for greasing

50g soft brown sugar

½ tsp freshly grated nutmeg

180g currants

4 tsp caster sugar, for dusting

special equipment

a 25cm round spring-form
cake tin

Make the enriched bread dough and leave it to rest, covered, in a warm place. After 15 minutes, dust your work surface with flour and place the dough on top. Knead for about 10 minutes, or until the dough feels smooth and satiny, then place it into a lightly oiled bowl, cover with a clean, dry tea towel and leave to rise for 1–1½ hours, or until almost doubled in size.

Meanwhile, make the filling by creaming together the butter, brown sugar and grated nutmeg until pale and fluffy. Add the currants and stir in well.

Grease the spring-form cake tin, line it with non-stick baking paper and set aside. When the dough is ready, place it on the lightly floured work surface and press out to a flat sheet. Using a rolling pin, roll to a rectangle about 30 x 35 cm, allowing the dough to rest for a few minutes if it shrinks back, then re-roll until you have the dimensions specified.

With the longest edge facing you, spread the filling mixture evenly over the entire surface of the dough then roll the dough up into a tight cylinder. Trim the edges to neaten the roll then, at 5cm intervals, cut through the dough to make 7 equal rounds. Arrange 6 of the rounds, flat-side down and evenly spaced apart, around the inside edge of the prepared tin and place the remaining round in the centre. Cover with cling film and leave to rise in a warm place for 30 minutes, or until the rounds have increased in size by about half and are beginning to push up against each other. Towards the end of the rising time preheat the oven to 160°C/gas mark 3.

Remove the cling film from the buns, dust them with 2 tsp caster sugar and bake for 20 minutes, or until the buns are golden brown. Once cooked, dust again with the remaining caster sugar, remove from the tin and cool before serving. Store for 2–3 days in an airtight tin or freeze for up to 1 month.

CORNISH SAFFRON BUNS

✳ Makes 8 buns ✳ Preparation time 3 hours including rising time ✳ Cooking time 15 minutes

10 saffron strands

1 quantity enriched dough (see page 69)

80g finely chopped homemade candied orange or grapefruit peel (see page 89)

for the glaze

1 egg yolk

1 tbsp milk

Place the saffron strands in a small bowl and add 1 tbsp boiling water and leave to cool.

Make the enriched bread dough as directed in the recipe, adding the saffron water to the sponge once it has developed. Add the candied peel with the remaining flour and mix to incorporate.

Place the dough on the work surface and knead for about 10 minutes, or until it feels soft, smooth and slightly tacky but not sticky. If it is too sticky, add a little flour as necessary while you knead. Shape the dough into a round and place it in a lightly oiled bowl. Cover with a clean, dry tea towel and leave to rise for 1–1½ hours, or until almost doubled in size.

Line a baking sheet with non-stick baking paper and set it aside. Place the dough onto the floured work surface and divide it evenly into 8 pieces weighing about 70g each. Shape each piece into a round ball and arrange, spaced about 4cm away from one another, on the prepared baking sheet. Cover loosely with cling film and leave in a warm place for approximately 30 minutes, or until almost doubled in size.

Towards the end of the rising time, preheat the oven to 180°C/gas mark 4. In a small bowl beat the egg yolk and milk together. Brush the top of the buns with the glaze and bake in the centre of the oven for 15 minutes, or until the buns are a deep golden brown and a probe inserted into the centre of a bun reads 95°C. Serve them warm with unsalted butter and lemon curd or honey. Store, when cold, in an airtight tin for up to 3 days, or freeze for up to 1 month.

LEMON SALLY LUNN

✳ Serves 6 ✳ Preparation time about 3 hours including rising time ✳ Cooking time 15–20 minutes

1 quantity enriched dough (see page 69)

finely grated zest of 1 lemon

for the glaze

2 tbsp caster sugar

zest and juice of 1 lemon

special equipment

a 20cm round spring-form cake tin and a temperature probe

Make the enriched bread dough. Mix in the lemon zest and leave the dough to rest, covered, in a warm place.

After 15 minutes, dust your work surface with flour, uncover the dough and place it on the work surface. Knead the dough for about 10 minutes, or until it feels smooth and satiny, then place it into a lightly oiled bowl, cover with a clean, dry tea towel and leave to rise for 1–1½ hours, or until almost doubled in size.

Grease the cake tin, line it with non-stick baking paper and set it aside. Place the risen dough onto the floured work surface and gently press it down to de-gas it then shape it into a tight round ball. Place the ball into the prepared tin and let it rest for 5 minutes. Press the dough down so it only comes up as far as the edge of the tin then cover loosely with cling film. Leave it to rise for 30 minutes to 1 hour, or until the bun has doubled in size. Towards the end of the rising time preheat the oven to 160°C/gas mark 3.

Bake for 15–20 minutes. Meanwhile make the glaze by placing the sugar, lemon juice and zest and 2 tbsp water into a small pan over medium heat. Let simmer until it has reduced by one-third and is the consistency of light syrup.

When the surface of the bun is a deep golden brown or a temperature probe inserted in the centre reads 95°C the bun is finished. Remove it from the oven and, using a pastry brush, glaze the bun using up all of the syrup. Any excess will run into the tin and be absorbed by the bun. Cool the bun in the tin. To serve, cut into slices and sandwich with either whipped cream or butter and jam. Store in an airtight tin for 2–3 days, or freeze for up to 1 month.

PRESERVES

A Note on Preserves

When preserving, always use fruit and vegetables that are in the peak of their season. They will then be at their most flavourful and should be at their lowest price, and you may be able to buy them by the crate or box from pick-your-own farms, farmers' markets or greengrocers at a keen price. (It is always worth haggling when stocks are high.) Look for fruit and vegetables that are plump, fresh, unbruised and dry and avoid buying fruit that is over-ripe – even if it is labelled 'good for jamming'. Also avoid fruit that is under-ripe because its flavour will not have developed fully.

Preserving equipment

Pans: A large, heavy, stainless steel jam-making (or maslin) pan is essential for home jam-making. Most of the pans on the market are of 9-litre capacity, with graded metric and imperial measurements on the inside. Buy one with two handles for ease of pouring. Aluminium pans are not suitable for making most preserves because the metal is easily dissolved by the fruit acids and vinegars you will be using.

Jam funnels: A wide-necked jam funnel is very useful when transferring hot preserves into jars. These can be metal or silicone. Before using, sterilise them in boiling water for two or three minutes.

Jars: Any modern glass jars should be suitable for preserves, but they will need to withstand temperatures of up to 120°C, because they must be sterilised in a low oven before use. Jar lids with rubberised seals must be boiled for 2–3 minutes to sterilise them. Kilner jars with rubber seals and clasps are excellent for this purpose.

Whatever you use, it is important to get a good seal to prevent drying out or spoilage. Metal lids are not appropriate for most preserves because fruit acids and vinegars will dissolve the metal. Plastic lids can be used, as can waxed-paper discs and cellophane, so long as they are secured well with string or an elastic band.

Ladles and spoons: Ladles and spoons for making jam must be scrupulously clean and non-absorbent to avoid any cross-contamination of flavours from other food. It is a goodidea to keep your jam-making equipment separate and only use it for that purpose. A heatproof, silicone spatula is very useful for scraping out the pan.

Quantities

When first making preserves, only attempt to make a small quantity. Jams and jellies in particular are best made in quantities of no more than one kilogram at a time so that they come to a boil quickly, preserving more of the fruit flavour and colour. If you find yourself faced with a large glut of fruit, work with two pans at once. One pan can be used to warm the fruit and dissolve the sugar, while the jam in the other pan is finishing. This way, you can easily make a series of small batches.

Setting jams and jellies

The individual recipes included in this chapter include many of the techniques commonly used when making preserves. The method for checking whether the setting point has been reached is the same for all jam and jelly recipes. Before beginning your jam or jelly, put one or two saucers in the fridge to cool, then follow the method described below:

Mixtures of fruit or fruit juices and sugar will come to a boil at a temperature over 100°C. As the water is driven off by boiling, the temperature will increase and the sugar concentration will rise. To test for temperature, make sure that your thermometer or probe is held in the main body of the jam. If it is held too near the bottom or top the reading will be inaccurate. As the mixture of fruit and sugar approaches 105°C, it will noticeably thicken, because at this point the pectin will begin to gel together to form a mesh. How long this takes depends on many factors, such as sugar content and acidity. You can see how far the pectin has meshed (in other words, if the jam or jelly has reached a setting point), by using the cold-saucer test.

To test for a set, spoon a small amount of the mixture onto one of the cold saucers you have placed in the fridge. Let it sit for a minute, then push the edge with your finger. You should notice that the surface wrinkles. If it does not, continue to cook the jam for a couple of minutes and then test it on a cold saucer again.

If the jam reaches a temperature above 107°C and has not yet reached a setting point, remove it from the heat. You can ladle it into the jars at this point but you will find that your jam does not set perfectly. If you prefer, you can add additional lemon juice, which is high in pectin, in the ratio of 1 lemon for each 500g of fruit in the initial mixture, then reboil. After adding the lemon juice, you should find that the jam sets. If you use jam sugar, which also contains added pectin, you should find that the jam sets every time without the addition of extra lemon juice.

SEVILLE ORANGE MARMALADE

✳ Makes approx 3kg marmalade – 6 to 8 jars ✳ Preparation time 1 hour 30 minutes
✳ Cooking time 2 hours 30 minutes to soften peel plus 1 hour to finish

Mrs Beeton was keen on both the bitter Seville orange, with its sharp juice and aromatic zest, and its sweet cousin – using them both widely in her preserves. The intensity of the Seville is unmatched, though, and this makes it superb for making marmalade.

1.4kg Seville oranges

2.8kg preserving sugar

1 lemon, sliced

special equipment

a stainless steel preserving pan, a muslin square and a sugar thermometer or temperature probe

Place the oranges in a large stainless steel pan with 3 litres of water, bring to a boil, then simmer the fruit gently for 2½ hours or until its skin is tender and the water has reduced to about 2.5 litres.

Remove the oranges to a colander set over a large bowl to catch the drips, and reserve the liquid in the pan. Still over the colander, cut the oranges in half and scoop the pith, pulp and seeds out into a bowl, then slice and reserve the peel. You should end up with roughly 1.9 litres of juice, 700g of sliced peel and 625g of pulp and seeds. If your volume of juice is less than this, add some cooking water to make up the difference.

Place 2 saucers in the fridge to chill for testing the set, and put your clean jars in a cool oven, 120°C/gas mark ½. Return the liquid and peel to the pan. Wrap the pith, pulp, seeds and sliced lemon in a muslin square, tie securely and drop that into the pan too. Over a high heat, simmer for 10 minutes until the peel is tender. Add the sugar, stirring well until fully dissolved, and then bring to a rapid boil over a high heat. Continue stirring frequently until the mixutre reaches 105° or starts to thicken, then test for the setting point using the cold-saucer method on page 81.

Remove the pan from the heat and allow the marmalade to stand for 10 minutes to form a skin, so that the peel will not rise when it is put into jars. Remove and discard any scum, then pot the marmalade into the warm jars, cover the surface with a disc of waxed paper and seal with cellophane. Store in a cool, dark place and use within 1 year of making.

BERRY JAM

✳ Makes approx 1.5kg – 3 or 4 jars ✳ Preparation time 10 minutes ✳ Cooking time 15 minutes

This recipe works well with strawberries, raspberries or brambles. For the best flavour it should only be made with dry, ripe fruit in peak season. Make only as much as you will eat in a month or two, as lightly set jams like this one do not keep forever. Mrs Beeton added redcurrant juice to her berry jams for its pectin and acidity, but a little lemon juice and jam sugar, used in combination, make a delicious jam that should set quickly.

900g fruit, stalks removed

750g jam sugar

2 tbsp lemon juice

special equipment

a stainless steel preserving pan and a sugar thermometer or temperature probe

Heat the oven to 120°C/gas mark ½ and place your clean jars on a baking sheet in the oven. Place a couple of saucers in the fridge for testing the set.

Chop the berries in half if they are large, then mix the fruit, sugar and lemon juice in a large stainless steel pan. Place the pan over a medium heat and stir gently as the fruit begins to release its juice. After 2 or 3 minutes turn the heat to high and scrape any sugar back from the sides of the pan into the mix. Boil rapidly for 3–4 minutes, stirring continuously to prevent the jam burning on the bottom of the pan.

When the temperature of the fruit has reached 105°C and the mixture begins to thicken, start testing for setting point using the cold-saucer method on page 81.

When it is ready, remove from the heat and allow the jam to form a skin. Remove and discard any scum that has formed, then pot the jam into the warm, sterilised jars. Cover the surface of the jam with a waxed-paper disc and seal the jar with cellophane.

Note: For a jam that will keep for longer, use equal quantities of sugar and fruit. The higher sugar content helps prevent fermentation or the growth of moulds. Note that preserving sugar and jam sugar are not the same thing. Jam sugar has added pectin, which encourages jam to set even with a limited boiling time; preserving sugar is simply a clear form of white sugar, all the better for making preserves.

BLACKCURRANT JAM

✳ Makes approx 1.5kg – 3 or 4 jars ✳ Preparation time 30 minutes ✳ Cooking time 20 minutes

When they are in their peak season, in the middle of July, you will find blackcurrants in farm shops and markets. Carefully pick the berries from their stems and remove any greenish berries before weighing the fruit and proceeding with the jam. This jam has an intense flavour and is a good keeper.

1kg blackcurrants

750g jam sugar

special equipment

a stainless steel preserving pan and a sugar thermometer or temperature probe

Heat the oven to 120°C/gas mark ½ and place your clean jars on a baking sheet in the oven. Put a couple of saucers in the fridge for testing the set.

Place the blackcurrants in a stainless steel pan with 200ml water and bring to a gentle simmer over a low heat for approximately 5 minutes, until the fruit breaks down. Add the sugar and stir until it has dissolved.

Turn up the heat and bring the fruit to a rolling boil, stirring constantly to prevent it catching.

Boil rapidly for 3–4 minutes, and when the temperature of the fruit has reached 105°C and the mixture begins to thicken, start testing for setting point using the cold-saucer method on page 81.

When the jam is ready, remove it from the heat and allow the jam to form a skin. Remove and discard any scum that has formed, then pot the jam into the warm, sterilised jars. Cover the surface of the jam with a waxed-paper disc and seal the jar with cellophane.

APRICOT JAM

✳ Makes 1.5 kg – 3 or 4 jars ✳ Preparation time 15 minutes ✳ Cooking time 25 minutes

There is more than a hint of high summer in this wonderful jam. Mrs Beeton scented it with the kernels of the apricots, which impart a delicious bitter-almond flavour. It is well worth spending the minute or two it takes to extract the kernels from the stones. Pay particular attention to this jam as it cooks – the skins of the apricots have a habit of sticking to the bottom of the pan.

1kg fresh apricots

750g jam sugar

juice of 1 lemon

special equipment

a stainless steel preserving pan, a small hammer and a sugar thermometer or temperature probe

Heat the oven to 120°C/gas mark ½ and place your clean jars on a baking sheet in the oven. Put a couple of saucers in the fridge for testing the set.

Halve the apricots, reserving the stones. Place the fruit in a large stainless steel pan with the jam sugar, lemon juice and 200ml water. Stir gently to amalgamate and leave to sit for 5 minutes.

Meanwhile, using a small hammer, break 10 of the stones and release the kernels. Place these in a small pan of water and bring to the boil. Cook for 2 minutes, then drain and cool in a bowl of cold water. Skin the kernels, chop finely and add to the pan of fruit.

Now place the large pan over a medium heat. Stir to dissolve the sugar into the fruit, then turn the heat up and bring to a rapid boil, stirring to prevent the apricot skins sticking to the bottom.

Boil the mixture rapidly for 3–4 minutes. When the jam has reached 105°C and begins to thicken, start testing for setting point using the cold-saucer method on page 81.

When the jam is ready, remove it from the heat and allow it to form a skin. Remove and discard any scum that has formed, then pot the jam into the warm, sterilised jars. Cover the surface of the jam with a waxed-paper disc and seal the jar with cellophane.

CANDIED PEEL

✳ Makes about 2kg ✳ Preparation time 20 minutes
✳ Cooking time approx 6 hours over 3 days plus 2 days air-drying

Although Mrs Beeton did not give a recipe for candied peel, it was listed as an ingredient in many of her cakes and puddings. Thick-skinned oranges and grapefruit, in particular, work excellently here. The resulting product is very sweet and can be stored when wet or after it has been dried. As candied peel takes a fair while to make, I would suggest that you make a large batch and then freeze it in small quantities for later use. If you would like to reduce the quantities in the recipe, it is easy to do – but keep the cooking times the same. Add this to many cake recipes in this book, or slice and dip in chocolate to make an excellent gift.

12 pink or red grapefruit or large oranges

3–4 kg granulated sugar

special equipment

a large stainless steel preserving pan

Make 2 cuts around each grapefruit at right angles allowing you to peel off the skin in 4 segments, leaving the fruit intact (you can eat this later). Place the peel in a large stainless steel pan. Cover with cold water, bring to the boil, and then discard the liquid. Repeat this process twice more, draining the peel after the third blanching. You will end up with about 1.5kg of blanched peel, depending on the size of the fruit.

Make the syrup by dissolving 2kg sugar in 2 litres of water. Add the peel, return to the heat and simmer very gently for approximately 2 hours, or until the peel is translucent and very tender. Remove from the heat and cool overnight.

The next day, transfer the peel to a bowl, measure the volume of the syrup and add sugar at the rate of 1kg per litre. Place over a medium heat and stir to dissolve the sugar, then increase the heat and bring to a rolling boil. Pour back over the peel and leave to cool overnight.

The next day, remove the peel and boil the syrup again, then pour back over the peel and again leave overnight to cool.

Once cooled, strain and arrange the peel on a wire cooling rack over a tray to catch drips. Allow it to dry at a warm room temperature for 2 days, until the peel begins to feel dry to the touch. Once it is absolutely dry, pack in sealed jars, filling up the space in between the slices with granulated sugar. If you prefer moist peel, it can be frozen instead.

LEMON CURD

✳ Makes approx 1.2kg – 3 or 4 jars ✳ Preparation time 20 minutes ✳ Cooking time 30 minutes

Although Mrs Beeton did not give a recipe for lemon curd as such, the filling for her lemon cheesecakes is effectively the same thing. To complete her recipe, simply spoon the curd into puff pastry cases in much the same way you would make jam tarts. This short-keeping preserve can also be used to fill a lemon sponge (see page 41) – simply mix with an equal quantity of lightly whipped double cream.

6–8 large, juicy lemons

225g unsalted butter

550g caster sugar

5 medium eggs and
2 egg yolks

special equipment

a large ceramic or heatproof
glass bowl

Place 3–4 clean jars on a baking sheet and into an oven heated to 120°C/gas mark ½.

Finely grate the zest of the lemons, then cut them in half and squeeze, straining the juice through a sieve into a bowl. Measure the juice: you need 250ml. If you have any excess, keep it in the fridge and use within 2 days.

Cut the butter into small pieces and place in a large ceramic or heatproof glass bowl over a pan of gently simmering water. Add the sugar and the lemon zest and juice, and stir with a wooden spoon until the sugar has completely dissolved.

Lightly beat the eggs and yolks and strain through a sieve into the mixture, stirring over a gentle heat to cook.

Continue to stir until the mixture thickens, which it will do at about 85°C, then remove it from the heat and pour into the warm jars. Cover the surface of the curd with a waxed-paper disc and seal the jar with cellophane.

Once cool, store in the fridge and use within 1 month.

LEMON MINCEMEAT

✳ Makes approx 2.8kg – about 6 jars ✳ Preparation time 15 minutes ✳ Cooking time 3 hours

Mrs Beeton's light, fresh lemon mincemeat is unusual in that it contains only currants – no raisins or other vine fruits such as you would find in most modern recipes. Along with the lemon, this gives a pleasant bitterness in contrast to the richness of the suet and spice.

**zest and juice of
2 large lemons**

**2kg Bramley cooking
apples, peeled, cored
and coarsely grated**

225g suet

450g currants

225g caster sugar

80g candied peel

2 tsp mixed spice

Preheat the oven to 120°C/gas mark ½.

Mix all the ingredients together in a large ovenproof dish until well combined. Transfer to a steel bowl or roasting tray, place in the preheated oven and cook, stirring occasionally, for 3 hours. Wash 6 jam jars and place them on a baking sheet in the oven with the mincemeat for the last half hour to sterilise them.

When the mixture has cooked, pot into the jars, covering the surface with a waxed-paper disc and sealing the jars with cellophane.

Keep in a cool, dark place for at least 2–3 months and then use within 1 year of making.

GLOSSARY OF COOKING TERMS

Many languages have influenced the British kitchen, but none so much as French – hardly surprising since French food has often been held up as the benchmark for excellence, in Mrs Beeton's time as well as in our own. Long before the Michelin guide began to report on British restaurants, French chefs were working for British royalty and could be found in the kitchens of many large country houses. Perhaps the most famous of these was Antonin Carême, chef to the Prince Regent (later George IV), who set the standard for future chefs to emulate. Mrs Beeton knew of him by name and reputation. The list below is intended to help explain the more commonly used terms – many, but not all, of which come from the French.

baking powder   a raising agent made from bicarbonate of soda and cream of tartar

beat   to mix food energetically to introduce air, using a wooden spoon, whisk or electric mixer to make a mixture light and fluffy

blend   to combine ingredients to give a smooth mixture

boil   to heat a liquid to the point at which it bubbles vigorously and begins to vapourise – 100°C in the case of water

caramel   a confection made by melting sugar. A simple caramel can be made by gently warming a mixture of sugar and water to 170–180°C, until the sugar melts and turns golden brown

chill   to cool food without freezing, usually in a refrigerator

compote   a dish of stewed fruit in sugar syrup, served cold

conserve   a sweet preserve usually made with whole fruits

consistency   texture, used to describe cakes and doughs

couverture   chocolate made especially for cooking, which contains a high proportion of cocoa butter. It has a glossier apprearance and is easier to handle than standard chocolate

crimp   to press pastry together decoratively, to seal

curdling   the process whereby fresh milk or sauce separates into solids and liquid. This can be intentional, as when making cheese, or unfortunate – for example when creamed butter and sugar split with the addition of eggs

dough   a mixture of flour, liquid and sometimes fat for baking into bread or cakes

dredge   to sprinkle food with flour or sugar

dust   to sprinkle lightly, for example with flour, sugar or spices

fold in   to combine ingredients carefully with a whisk, metal spoon or spatula in order to retain any air that has been incorporated into the mixutre

gelatine   a setting agent derived from the bones of animals, used for setting jellies

glaze   a glossy finish given to food, usually by brushing with beaten egg or milk before cooking, or with sugar syrup after cooking

gluten   the main protein component of some flours, notably wheat flours

infuse   to combine aromatic herbs and/or vegetables with a liquid such as stock or milk (or, in the case of tea making, water) and leave them for a period of time to impart their flavour

maslin pan   jam pan

meringue   a light mixture of beaten egg whites and sugar

nibbed   (of nuts, usually almonds) chopped

pectin   a gum-like substance which acts as a setting agent in jams and jellies. It is found naturally in some fruits and vegetables, notably lemons

preserve   to keep food in good condition by treating it with salt, vinegar or sugar

pulp   the soft, fleshy tissue of fruit or vegetables, or the result of cooking or mashing fruit

purée   food that has been blended or passed through a sieve to give a smooth texture

scald   to heat cream or milk to just below boiling point. Originally, the main purpose of this was to eliminate harmful bacteria and enzymes (which are no longer present in pasteurised milk), but other purposes include encouraging the growth of yeast when making bread, or helping other ingredients to infuse

setting point   the stage of cooking a jam or jelly at which it will set when cooled

sift   to pass flour or sugar through a sieve to remove any lumps and/or incorporate air

simmer   to cook in liquid that is kept just below boiling point

skim   to remove residue from the surface of a liquid, for example fat from stock or scum from jam

spring-form   describes a cake tin with hinged sides and a loose bottom

stir   to mix with a circular motion, using a spoon or fork

syrup   a sugar dissolved in water or another liquid

turnover   a savoury or sweet pastry made by folding a round or square of pastry in half over a filling, usually of fruit, forming a semicircle or triangle (see page 23)

vanilla sugar   sugar with a vanilla flavour, usually made by storing caster sugar with used vanilla pods in order to extract the oils

whip   to beat eggs or cream until they are thick and increased in volume

whisk   a looped wire utensil that is used to introduce air into ingredients such as eggs or cream

yeast   a fungus used to leaven bread

yoghurt   milk that has been cultured with bacteria, most commonly Lactobacillus

zest   the coloured outer skin of citrus fruits in which the highly flavoured oils are contained

INDEX

ACKNOWLEDGEMENTS

My childhood was filled with the smell of baking – both my grandmothers, Elsie and Nora, baked on Thursday morning, getting themselves and their homes ready for a weekend of meals and potential visitors. Everyday cakes and breads would be made as required, with special cakes for occasions. I learnt to enjoy – perhaps a little too much – the combination of butter, flour, sugar and eggs at their kitchen table, and for that I am ever thankful.

During the writing of this book, Mum, Sandra Baker, helped without question in the kitchen and office both in the process of testing the recipes and in organising manuscripts – you are a blessing.

To my sister Louise, and to Oscar and Fanny for providing moral support go hearty thanks. Much respect and love goes to Dad, John Baker, who makes a mean apple turnover.

Amanda Harris and Debbie Woska sat through the creation of *Mrs Beeton How to Cook* with me – providing just the right amount of support and encouragement – thank you. Zelda Turner deserves thanks for helping trim and sculpt the recipes in this smaller collection. To all the design team – Julyan Bayes, Lucie Steriker, Sammy-Jo Squire and her crew, and the photographer Andrew Hayes-Watkins and his team for making the book look so beautiful. The team behind the scenes at Orion helped enormously – Elizabeth Allen and Nicky Carswell especially.

So many of my friends love cake, but chief among them are my dear friends John and Clarinda Foster, who have provided me with so much support over the years.

Gerard Baker